THE JOY OF ORNAMENTATION

by
GIOVANNI LUCA CONFORTO

being Conforto's
TREATISE ON ORNAMENTATION (Rome, 1593)

with a Preface by
SIR YEHUDI MENUHIN

and an Introduction by
DENIS STEVENS

Pro/Am Music Resources, Inc.
White Plains, New York

In Roma con licentia de Superiori, et Priuileggio · 1 1 8 3

Copyright © 1989 by Denis Stevens. All rights reserved under International and Pan-American Copyright Conventions. Printed in the United States of America.

Books by Denis Stevens: *A History of Song* (Ed.; London, 1960; New York [Rev. 2nd Ed.,], 1970), *The Letters of Claudio Monteverdi* (Ed. & Transl.; London & New York, 1980), *Monteverdi: Sacred, Secular, and Occasional Music* (Teaneck & London, 1978), *The Mulliner Book: A Commentary* (London, 1952), *Music and Art in Society* (Ed. & Transl., with Sheila Stevens; University Park, 1968), *Musicology: A Practical Approach* (London & New York, 1980), *Musicology in Practice* (White Plains & London [2 vols.], 1987–1989), *The Pelican History of Music* (Ed., with Alec Robertson; Harmondsworth & New York [3 vols.], 1960–1968), *Thomas Tomkins, 1572–1656* (London, 1957; New York [Rev. 2nd Ed.], 1967), *Tudor Church Music* (New York, 1955; London [Rev. 2nd Ed.], 1961).

Published in the United States of America 1989 by
PRO/AM MUSIC RESOURCES, INC.
63 Prospect Street, White Plains, New York 10606
ISBN 0-912483-49-0

Published in Great Britain 1989 by
KAHN & AVERILL
9 Harrington Road, London SW7 3ES

Preface to the treatise on ornamentation by Giovanni Luca Conforto

We owe a great debt to musicologists these days and to their patient and detailed study of treatises and manuscripts in moulding libraries all over the world, for they have given us a whole new repertory and the means to do it justice. They have enabled us to live with and understand the subtle and passionate feelings, and, in fact, the very thoughts and the life of peoples and cultures preceding the romantic 19th century, of which we had been denied. I have a particular personal debt to Denis Stevens, for we have worked closely together for many years in connection with my Bath Festival and more recently on works by Tartini and Leclair. I have often consulted him on a wide range of musical subjects. This little preface to a book, which will be of inestimable value to me and my colleagues, comes as a tribute from my heart for a man whose erudition and charm I have long admired.

Yehudi Menuhin

INTRODUCTION

I HAVE ALWAYS RETAINED A SPECIAL AFFECTION FOR THIS LITTLE BOOK BY GIOVANNI LUCA CONFORTO, WHICH I FIRST CAME ACROSS AS A FACSIMILE edited by Johannes Wolf under the auspices of the Paul Hirsch Library and published, without my knowing, in the year of my birth. That splendid library, then in Frankfurt am Main, was later transported to England, going first to Cambridge and subsequently (through the generosity of its founder) to the British Library, where it has long since nourished the interests of countless scholars. I purchased my copy in 1948, while in Hamstead visiting Otto Haas's book-shop, soon to pass into the capable hands of my friend Albi Rosenthal.

It was not long before the book suddenly revealed a practical usefulness out of all proportion to its modest size, for in 1949 I was placed in charge of pre-classical music on the BBC's cultural wavelength, the Third Programme, begun in 1946 through the efforts of Sir William Haley and George Barnes. It was a time when (*pace* the latter-day lumpkins who maintain that the revival of early music began in 1972—or was it 1973?) a lively post-war interest in exploring the pre-Bach repertoire was not only sustained but amply rewarded by a corporation that prided itself on the proper educational use of public funds. Looking back over the years, I would call that particular time and place a musicologist's paradise (*et ego in Arcadia vixi?*) and by great good fortune I was the only such creature on the staff. Building and producing programmes was not unlike entering a vast and almost uninhabited treasure-house whose unimagined riches were waiting only to be transformed from the silent page to the resounding air.

Modern performances of vocal and instrumental music written between about 1550 and 1650 posed special problems for a producer. Neither in England nor anywhere else in the world was there then a school for the study and interpretation of music in accordance with known—but not generally understood—principles of ornamentation. Artists with a scholarly background, usually instrumentalists and very few in number, had some idea of what had to be done. Singers on the whole did not, since the art of ornamentation formed no part of their training either at colleges of music or in places where music might (in Ruskin's phrase) exalt and purify. So it was that late in September of 1949 I began to study Conforto's treatise with the idea of introducing the principles and practices advocated by its author some three and a half centuries previously.

Suddenly the historical remoteness vanished as singer after singer began to grapple with the various roulades and ornaments, slowly absorbing and mastering them as Conforto said they could. This process of familiarization went on for three years, covering many aspects of early repertory, some of which were until then almost completely unknown. Then in 1952 I produced two studio performances of Monteverdi's *Orfeo*, with a cast of singers including Pierre Bernac in the title role, Alfred Deller, Irma Kolassi, Ilse Wolf, Jennifer Vyvyan, Norman Walker, Mary Jarred, Martin Lawrence, Bruce Boyce and Wilfred Brown. The conductor was Walter Goehr, who enthusiastically seconded my proposal that we incorporate suitable vocal ornamentation from Conforto's treatise. Although these performances are not well documented in books on the composer or his earliest masterpiece, I can vouch for the fact that in matters of ornamentation, realization of continuo, and the solving of rhythmic problems the "Orfeo project" was far ahead of its time.

Subsequent experiments showed that the method worked, and worked well, for it was not more difficult to grasp than many later subtleties of interpretation. In 1958 I mentioned the book in a paper given at the Cologne Congress of the International Musicological Society, and this was subsequently published in the official Congress Report (Kassel, 1959, pp.284-287). But still I could not find a publisher willing to re-issue this potentially useful tool, and in consequence the idea was shelved indefinitely.

* * * * * *

A BUMP ON THE WESTERLY SIDE OF ITALY'S FOOT MARKS THAT REGION OF CALABRIA WHERE, ALONG ROUTE 18 BETWEEN VIBO VALENTIA AND ROSARNO, WE pass the small and still rather remote town of Mileto, beloved of Count Roger of Sicily, who died there in 1101 and was buried in the abbey of S. Trinità which he himself had founded. Not a particularly lively or likely place, perhaps, for the emergence of a virtuoso falsettist who at the age of twenty was already a member of the Papal Chapel; yet he may have received his early musical education at the abbey, eventually travelling northwards in search of greater opportunities.

At the end of October 1585, after five years with the Papal Chapel, Conforto was expelled, but within a few weeks his services were being keenly sought after by the Gonzaga's man in Rome, Paolo Faccone, who was in close touch with the Apostolic Protonotary Capilupi and Scipione Gonzaga, recently appointed Patriarch of Jerusalem and a founder-member of the Accademia degli Invaghiti. Guglielmo Gonzaga, Third Duke of Mantua, was determined to lure to his court the finest artists available, knowing perhaps that he had but a year to live. His agents therefore busied themselves in seeking out and listening to vocalists and instrumentalists recommended by the composer Giovanni Maria Nanino, at that time in charge of the music at S. Maria Maggiore. This renowned composer and director affirmed that Conforto was the best singer available, both for sacred and secular music, also that he appeared to be a charming and modest man.

After leaving the Papal chapel, Conforto appears to have given himself a nineteen-month sabbatical until May 1587 when he was hired by Ruggiero Giovanelli, director of music at San Luigi dei Francesi.[1] Prior to that appointment his free time was put to the best possible use. Freelance

---

1   I am grateful to my daughter Daphne Stevens Pascucci for finding and copying Alberto Cametti's article (see Bibliography). In it he states that the singer had a one-year contract at the end of which he was given the option either to sing regularly or to resign. Conforto chose the latter course and left at the end of April 1588.

musicians, in Rome more than anywhere else, could make considerable sums of money by singing not only in dozens of churches and private chapels, but also in private concerts organized for the benefit of the cardinals who vied with each other in the splendor of their musical offerings. (Monteverdi, in Venice, would sometimes earn a fee equivalent to one-fifth of his annual salary for just one engagement.) Conforto was in the same class or better, for as everyone knows a virtuoso singer could then, and still can, easily outdo a composer in matters of high finance.

One of the most exciting and successful series of Lenten concerts in Rome was that of S. Trinità dei Monti, a late fifteenth-century monastery church soaring above the Piazza di Spagna and flanked by the Villa Medici and the Capuchin Church of S. Maria della Concezione. The finest musicians in Rome gathered together there, and attendance was never less than squeezing full. Capilupi took Scipione Gonzaga along one evening when the famous Giovanni Battista (known as Giacometti) was playing the violin and Giovanni Luca Conforto was singing, and the next day he wrote to Duke Guglielmo: "Giovanni Luca is better than just average — he sings with head voice, invents descants, and makes his embellishments sound like the nightingale itself. Some would prefer greater delicacy, but in chamber music he succeeds very well and cultivates a In this kind of music he sings falsetto, and is the best in Rome. In church he sings contralto, joining with all sorts of instruments. He can extemporize as well as sing by heart."

But on hearing of the Mantuan offers for the services of Giovanni Battista del Violino (Giacometti), Conforto felt slighted and promptly withdrew from the negotiations. Years later Pietro della Valle (who heard Conforto sing in the very early years of the seventeenth century) said that "he could sing as high as the heavens" (*Discorso della musica dell'età nostra,* Rome, 1640). Perhaps the penny-pinching Gonzaga lost an irreplaceable artistic bargain. Years later, around 1628, Vincenzo Giustiniani, a Genoese nobleman and connoisseur of the arts then living in Rome — where his brother, Cardinal Benedetto Giustiniani, was host to many famous musicians — wrote a *Discorso sopra la musica* which adopts a somewhat critical stance in regard to Conforto's excesses of ornamentation, and it may well be that some found him over-enthusiastic in promoting his own specialty.

Giustiniani also mentions Conforto in connection with Ferrara, and although there is some doubt about this, it does seem that he was among the singers accompanying the Papal household when it journeyed to Ferrara at the time of the crisis over the Este succession in the spring of 1598. By coincidence the Archduke Ferdinand was visiting the city for the first two weeks of May, and attended a solemn Te Deum which was followed by several motets sung by the Papal choir.[2]

Conforto was once more engaged as a singer in the Papal chapel in November 1591. He had contributed a canzonetta *Amara vita è quella* to Paolo Quagliati's Second Book of Canzonette (1588), and edited a collection of liturgical music in 1592. In the following year we have his *Breve e facile maniera,* in 1601 his *Salmi passeggiati,* and in 1607 a similar work, the *Passaggi sopra tutti li salmi,* on the title page of which he is still described as a singer in the Papal chapel. He continued and developed a tradition that was still alive more than two centuries later when Mendelssohn visited Rome and heard the Holy Week ceremonies. Writing to Carl Friedrich Zelter on 16 June 1831, he explains that: "The psalms are chanted *fortissimo* by all the male voices of the two choirs.... All the words, except that last, are sung with extreme rapidity on one note, but on the last they make a short 'melisma' which is different in the first and second verse." And later on in the same letter: "The chief soprano, Mariano, came from the mountains to Rome especially to sing on this occasion, and it is to him I owe hearing the *embellimenti* with their highest notes."

Although the date of Conforto's death is not so far known, his career lasted sufficiently long to enable him to make a considerable impression on Roman musical life at one of its most splendid epochs. He may have

---

2   Theophil Antonicek, "*Italienische Musikerlebnisse Ferdinands II. 1598*", in *Anzeiger der phil.- hist. Klasse der Österreichischen Akademie der Wissenschaften,* Jahrgang 1967, 102.

returned, in old age, to the town of his birth with its fine old abbey church. Was he thinking of it, perhaps, when he chose the Marian antiphon sung from Trinity to Advent for his vocalized syllables in the first few pages? Even fragmented, they make some sense, for away in Rome he was an exile: *Salve [Regina], Mater [misericordiae. Vita, dulcedo, et spes nostra] Salve. Ad te clamamus exules....* And was it he who chose the engraving of Orpheus for the verso of his title-page? Johannes Wolf and others who followed his lead considered the seated figure with lira da braccio to be Apollo. But the Greeks thought of Apollo as a terrible, fearsome and death-dealing god, and only secondarily as a poet and musician. He is usually depicted as tall, beardless, standing alone; and the animals sacred to him included the griffin, hawk, cock, grasshopper, lizard, crow and wolf. None of them appears in this engraving.

Conforto's unknown artist shows us a peaceful, thoughtful man seated by a tree. Around him birds and animals listen contentedly and even the serpent destined to kill his future wife Eurydice writhes itself into the shape of a C-clef. Shakespeare reminds us that the divine musician calmed not only the forest creatures, for

> Orpheus with his lute made trees
> And the mountain-tops that freeze,
> Bow themselves when he did sing.

Of the many artistic representations of Orpheus, most have a great deal in common with this charming figure. One thinks of the bas-relief Orpheus in Giotto's Florentine campanile, or the pavement of St. Catherine's chapel in the church of San Domenico in Siena. Even a simple engraving like that of Bartolomeo Montagna stresses the essentially tranquilizing effect of this magical *al fresco* concert.

It nearly escaped from us, for only three copies are known to survive: two in the British Library, and one in Bologna (Conservatorio). As may be seen, the type used for the date was very worn, so for years it was given as "1593–?1603". The former, now generally adopted, is by far the more convincing of the two.

*   *   *   *   *   *

CONFORTO MAY HAVE BEEN A GOOD TEACHER, BUT HIS WRITTEN ACCOUNT OF "THE METHOD"[3] IS COUCHED IN SUCH TURGID PROSE AS TO MAKE ONE WONDER whether he read the *Hypnerotomachia Poliphili* at breakfast every morning. The best solution here is to summarize, following this with a brief and (I hope) succinct *modus operandi*. In some ways I regret having to change the format from landscape to portrait, but his was a pocket book while the present edition is mainly for study as a prelude to practice. Since two of his original pages now combine to make one, there are fifteen pages instead of the original thirty. He begins numbering the music on page 3, with page 4 as the verso; these together correspond to my page 17.

His opening flourish is pure and unadulterated sales talk: "They laughed when I sat down to ornament." Only in princely courts and big cities can you hear ornamentation properly performed, and even then the practitioners are more often than not imported. After much thought he has decided to write a brief method, so that singers can learn the basics of ornamentation in just two months. He has set down passages useful in many ways — to beautify and embellish a melody, and to help make the voice (or hand) more flexible. Although the main thrust of the method is vocal, he does say at the end that instrumentalists can also benefit, and this is perfectly true except for the fact that they will not want to practice the *trillo*.

Looking at the first page (17), the choice of clefs is self-explanatory. The little cross in lines 1, 2 and 6 is a time-saver: if you don't wish to plow through the whole page, the three most suitable passages are marked with a cross. If you see a note with no tail (middle one of the three-note "chord" in bar 1) it has the same value as those above and below. With three transitional notes to choose from, the singer enjoys more variety.

---

3   Reproduced as an Appendix, below.

All that the student needs to do is move from B to C, assuming the treble clef has been selected, suitable for sopranos and tenors. The five possible moves in bar 1 (with various harmonies) are as follows:

Conforto's explanation omits No. 3 (his No. 4). In the penultimate line, a "3" introduces variations in *minor hemiola* or triple meter, and as before the number of notes is doubled as the examples proceed. He also draws attention here to a different use of the "3" meaning *trillo* (rapid repetition of one and the same pitch) but this does not begin to rear its tweeny head until the first bar of page 25.

After rising a step, the next section (page 18) deals with the very useful and important matter of falling a step. The old "tenor cadence" of earlier times is now typical of cadential movement in the uppermost voice, and not only is it typical, it is of frequent occurrence. For this very reason variety is called for if we wish to avoid boredom, and here Conforto's numerous and ingenious variants for the descent of a tone or semitone are of particular interest. The following example from Monteverdi's *Il ballo delle ingrate* show how two of the formulae can be applied to cadences on A and G:

The sections involving leaps down a fourth or up a fifth ("*salto di quarta in giù*"; "*salto di quinta in su*", and their opposites) begin three lines from the bottom of page 20, continuing to page 23. Conforto is here concerned with the student's knowledge of harmony, i.e. the bass that lies below the two notes. Faulty consonances and consecutive fifths should be avoided, but these considerations should cause no undue hardship nowadays. In a very wordy exegesis he explains that the different roulades within one and the same bar are meant to provide some choice when there is a problem of vocal range.

He then goes on to say that since there are far too many cadenzas to write out, he will give enough examples to provide an adequate variety, and that they may be used to embellish madrigals and arias, as well as for unaccompanied singing. A very useful selection of ornaments is shown on page 28, beginning with upper trills, long and short, followed by the *trillo* also in long and short forms. Giovanni Battista Doni, in his *Trattato della musica scenica* (reprinted by A. Solerti in *Le origini del melodramma,* Turin, 1903) calls it a "rippling, vibration, of the voice — *un increspamento (vibratio) di voce* — taken perhaps from the nightingale, and this does not audibly change the pitch." Conforto himself was compared to that musical song-bird. So, unlike modern vibrato, which too often changes the pitch in an unpleasant fashion, the old ornament referred to by Sebastien Brossard as "*le véritable trillo à l'Italienne*" does not noticeably wobble. The Germans called it *Bockstriller* — goat's trill — and this is what it may have sounded like in the hands, or rather the throats, of unskilled performers. One of the best among recent investigations is that of Carol MacClintock in her article "Caccini's *Trillo*—a Reexamination", in *Bulletin of the National Association of Teachers of Singing,* XXXIII (1976), 38-44.

The term *groppo* describes our trill, with an auxiliary note beaten above the principal note ("*di sopra*") or below ("*di sotto*"). Other kinds of cadential figures, half-bar and full bar, are given in the last four lines of page 26. Conforto always stresses the options open to the student, in that note-values can be changed as needed, and if attention is paid to his manner of setting out exercises the basic techniques can be learned in just over a week. (Alice-like, the time-plan of his lessons seems to lessen as the pages are turned.) But to commit these figures to memory may take three weeks.

A good piece of advice he gives is to consider carefully the nature of the notes to be ornamented and (most important) their suitability for embellishment. He also advocates the development of taste, by learning to distinguish between the excellent and the tawdry. This can be achieved by assiduous practice, and by listening carefully and critically to other singers and players. He omits to mention an ornament that was known in his time but not fully exploited until slightly later, and that is the *ribattuto della gola,* by which a short trillo is introduced by a dotted-note passage in which auxiliary notes beat against the main one, as in this excerpt from Monteverdi's *Combattimento:*

Now: to create your masterpiece of embellishments, take a piece of music paper, and write on it the intervals or cadences you wish to decorate, leaving sufficient space after each one for the desired cadenza.

Next, assuming your first interval is a leap down a third, turn to the lowest stave on page 19 (Giovanni's page 8). You have six staves full of extremely varied ornamental passages. When you have tried them over, choose the one you want and copy it out next to the interval already written down.

Now cut it out and paste (gum, glue, or tape) it in its proper place in the copy you are using for performance.

Proceed to the next sample, following previous instructions as above.

* * * * * *

Perhaps the most remarkable musico-poetical commentary on the art of vocal ornamentation is that of Guarini and Monteverdi in the poem entitled *Gorga di cantatrice*—"*Mentre vaga Angioletta*", in which every known trick of the voice is described with insight and skill:

E la volve e la spinge
con rotti accenti et con ritorti giri,
qui tarda e là veloce;
e talor mormorando
in basso e mobil suono ed alternando
fughe e riposi e placidi respiri.
Or la sospende e libra
or la preme, or la frange, or la raffrena,
or la saetta e vibra,
or in giro la mena...

She turns it around and urges it on
With broken accents and with twisted turns,
Here slowly, there fast;
And sometimes murmuring in deep and moving sound,
And alternating flights with repose and peaceful breathing.
Now she suspends it and frees it,
Now presses, breaks it, slows it down,
Now she shoots it and lets it vibrate,
Now leads it around...

As set by Monteverdi in his Eighth Book of Madrigals (1638) this tribute to Angioletta, a virtuoso singer of the time, takes on a new and positive meaning. I am still haunted by what was possibly its first recording, by Wilfred Brown and Gerald English, tenors, on a Vanguard record (BGS 5007), made in 1957. I can only hope that singers will study this book and learn to produce and project ornaments that have something of that "first fine careless rapture" of the late Renaissance and early Baroque.

DENIS STEVENS
Santa Barbara, 1989

BIBLIOGRAPHY

Berlotti, Antonio. *Musica alla corte dei Gonzaga in Mantova dal secolo XV al XVIII.* Milan, 1890.

Brown, Howard M. *Instrumental Music Printed Before 1600.* Cambridge MA, 1965.

Cametti, Alberto. "G.L. Conforto, falsettista del '500", *Musica,* XII, 15 March 1918, Rome.

Canal, Pietro. *Della musica in Mantova: notizie tratte principalmente dall'Archivio Gonzaga.* Venice, 1881.

Fenlon, Iain. *Music and Patronage in Sixteenth-Century Mantua.* Cambridge, 1980.

Ferand, Ernst T. *Die Improvisation in der Musik.* Zurich, 1938.

Kuhn, M. *Die Verzierungskunst in der Gesangsmusik des 16. bis 17. Jahrhunderts.* Leipzig, 1902.

Lach, Robert. *Studien zur Entwicklungsgeschichte der ornamentalen Melopöie.* Leipzig, 1913.

MacClintock, Carol (Transl.). *Hercole Bottrigari: "Il desiderio"; Vincenzo Giustiniani: "Discorso sopra la musica".* n.p., 1962.

Newcomb, Anthony. *The Madrigal at Ferrara, 1579-1597.* Princeton, 1980.

Stevens, Denis. *Musicology: A Practical Guide.* London and New York, 1980.

Wolf, Johannes (Ed.). *G.L. Conforto: Breve et facile maniera.... Im Faksimile mit Übersetzung herausgegeben.* Berlin, 1922.

GIOVANNI LUCA CONFORTO

TREATISE ON ORNAMENTATION

(Rome, 1593)

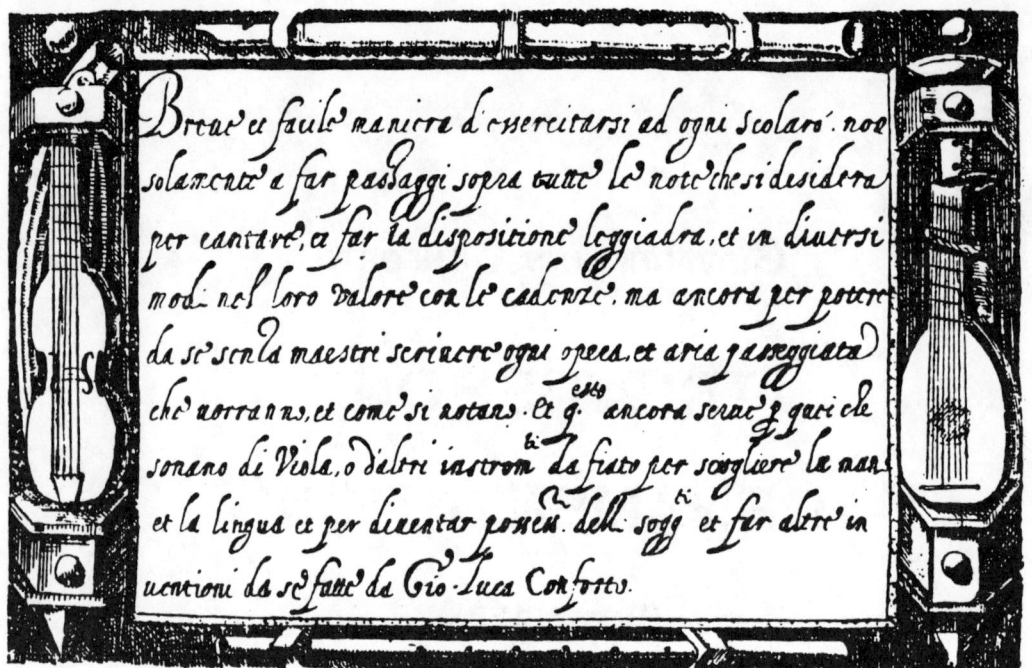

"Breve et facile maniera d'essercitarsi ad ogni scolaro, non solamente a far passaggi sopra tutte le note che si desidera per cantare, et far la dispositione leggiadra, et in diversi modi nel loro valore con le cadenze, ma ancora per potere da se senza maestri scrivere ogni opera, et aria passeggiata che vorrano, et come si notano. Et q[u]esto ancora serve p[er] quei che sonano di Viola, o d'altri instrom[en]ti da fiato per sciogliere la man et la lingua et per diventar possess[o]ri delli sogg[et]ti et far altre inventioni da se fatte da Gio[vanni] Luca Conforto."

"A brief and easy method for every student not only to perform ornaments on all the notes he wishes to sing, and make them sound attractive in various ways in their duration, with cadences; but also to be able, on his own, without teachers, to ornament any work, or aria as required, and as written down. This will also prove useful to those who play the Viola, or wind instruments, for loosening the hand and tongue, and to become possessors of these motives and make up other inventions of their own... by Giovanni Luca Conforto."

THE MUSIC

Conforto's [JOY OF] ORNAMENTATION (1593)

Conforto's [JOY OF] ORNAMENTATION (1593)

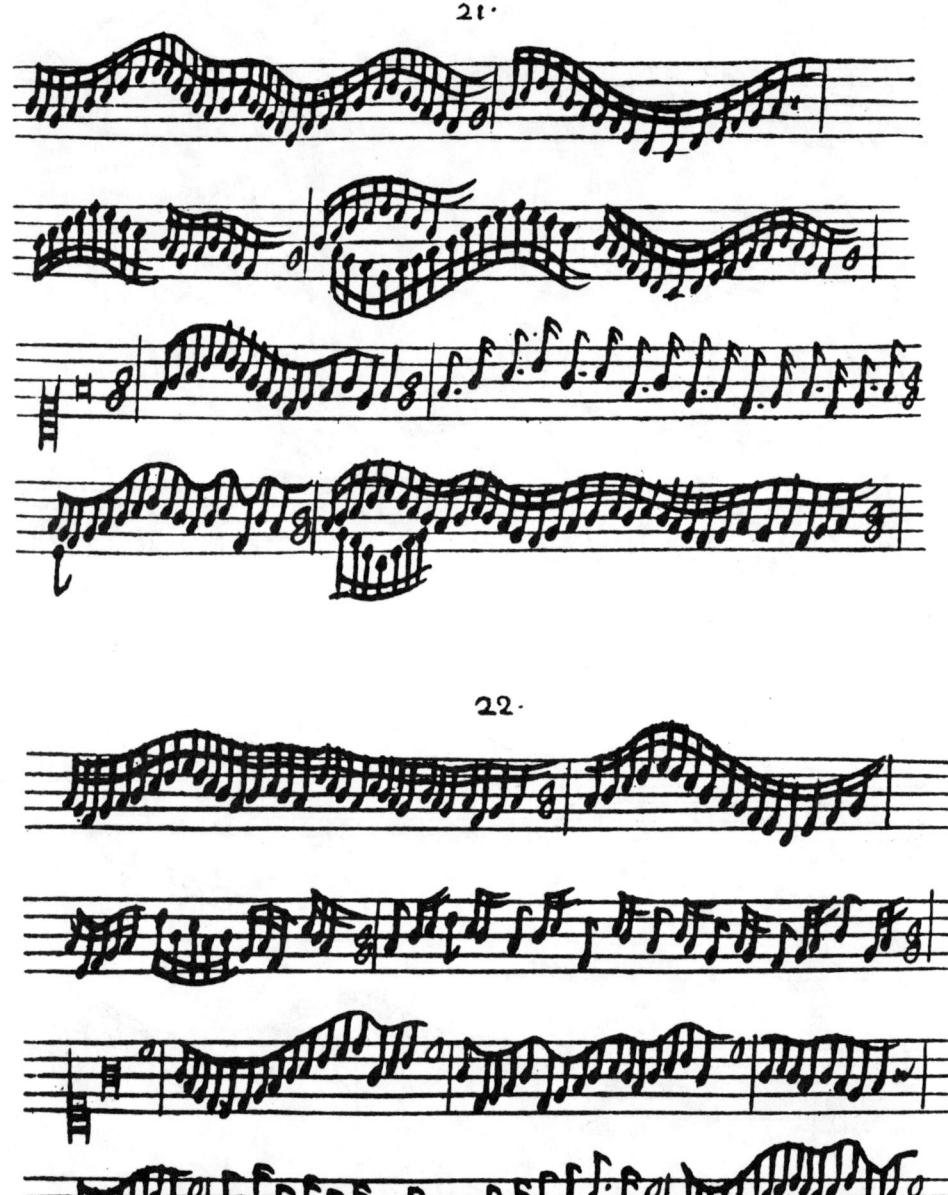

APPENDIX

DICHIARATIONE
SOPRA LI PASSAGGI
DI GIO. LVCA CONFORTI.

ALLI LETTORI.

Essendomi accorto, che solo ndle Città grandi, & nelle corti de Prencipi, si vsa il modo di cantar cõ vaghezza, e dispositione, & che quelli che in ciò hanno riportato lode, sono stati, per lo più, virtuosi, non in esse nati, ma forestieri iui trasportati, li quali hanno acquistata per prattica, solo per sentire in progresso di molto tempo, & senza regola: & hauend'io osseruato, che tutti quelli che cantano, & sonano, non hanno speranza d'acquistarla, se non con molta difficoltà, & lungo tempo, hò meco pensato più volte, come si potesse ad vtilità cõmune trouar modo da scemar questa fatica; & in fine, mi è venuto in mente, che forse ciò si potesse esseguire con vna maniera breue, con la quale potranno tutti quelli, che cantano, in meno di duoi mesi, far acquisto di bona, & leggiadra dispositione.

Così mi son indotto à far la presente regola, & à mettere insieme questi Passaggi, che in molti & diuersi modi si possono vsare per far la dispositione cantando sopra tutte le note ferme: & per compiacere à gl'amici, & per giouare à chi desidera di cantar bene, & per leuare à me la fatica di farne più copie; mi è parso mandarli in luce: & per fuggir la grandezza del volume, ho preso solamente quelli che à mio giuditio sono più gratiosi, e diletteuoli, & questi hò cercato di ridurli à più facilità, & breuità che sia possibile, come si vede l'vno à canto, & dentro all'altro, in vna istessa casella.

Hora dico, che tutte le chiaui, che nelle righe della prima imposta si veggono, fanno variare di nome, il soggetto, & il passaggio, & nelle altre righe restano in bianco, da farsi à beneplacito di quelli, che si esserciteranno nelle voci à loro più commode: douendosi intendere, che si come per la chiaue di Gesolreut, si dice mi fà, così anco nell'istesso luogo, perda diuersità de gl'altri, può dire, vt re, fa sol, sol la, & il simile per descendenza, per terza, quarta, & quinta.

Quanto alle note di paſſaggio, ſe alcune ſono ſenza coda, vagliono pur come le altre, che li ſtanno appreſſo; & la collocatione dell'vna ſopra l'altra, moſtra in quanti modi ſi può variare il paſſaggio.

Per eſſempio, ſono ſoprapoſte tre note nella prima caſella, le quali per la chiaue di Geſolreut ſopra il primo ſoggetto, vuole che ſi dica mi fà: adunque le variationi dicono, mi la ſol mi fà, & queſto è il primo modo: il ſecondo è, mi fà ſol mi fà: il terzo, mi fà re mi fà: il quinto, mi la re mi fà, l'iſteſſa regola ſi oſſeruarà nell'altre caſelle, ſe ben ſaranno di crome, ò ſemicrome.

La parola Salue, con altre che vi ſono, ſi poſſono eſſercitare in cambio di dire le note, per aſſuefare le vocali à far la diſpoſitione.

Il ſegno del tre, doue ci ſono tre ſemiminime, che ne ſiegue poi ſei crome, & dodici ſemicrome alla battuta, è chiamata generalmente emiola minore, & porta ſeco il valore delle triple, conforme al loro genere, di tre note alla battuta.

L'altro tre, che ſi vede ſotto duoi crome, ouero nel fine delle cadenze, altro non voglio dire che trillo, che rendendo al doppio il numero, imbelliſce il canto, & copre molti difetti.

Il ſalto che ſi vede della prima alla ſeconda nota, per quarta & quinta delli paſſaggi, coſì di ſotto, come di ſopra, non occorre dichiararlo à quelli che non hanno cognitione delle conſonanze; & quelli che ne hanno intelligenza, conoſcono, che la prima nota del paſſaggio con il baſſo, è ſpecie di quinta, facendoſi il ſalto di quarta in ſù, & la ſeconda è ottaua; & eſſendo il ſalto di quinta pur in ſù, e ſpecie di ottaua, & l'altra è duodecima, & ſaltando di ſotto, ogn'vna di eſſe torna al ſuo luogo; concedendo l'iſteſſe regola alla parte del baſſo, fuor che il ſalto della quinta.

Et l'eſſere in più modi il paſſaggio in vna iſteſſa caſella, ſono fatti per quelli, che haueſſero difficultà d'andare alto, ò baſſo con la voce, e con la diſpoſitione, cioè che nell'incominciare il paſſaggio vi ſono alcuni che vanno con la diſpoſitione più volentieri in ſù, che in giù, ò più in giù, che in ſù.

Et per non faſtidire, hò fatto poche cadenze, & delle più ordinarie col baſſo, poiche le diuerſità di eſſe ſarebbono molte, & non occorreua ſcriuerle, poiche ſon paſſaggiate tutte le note che potrebbono formare non ſolamente li paſſaggi per paſſaggiare madrigali & arie, ma anco le cadenze per cantare ſolo, ò accompagnato, & vi hò poſto il fà ſol di meza battuta, che ſerue per fine di eſſe cadenze, & anco per l'altre note che concludono, come il fà ſol, ſol la, mi fà, & altre. Et ſe bene le note, che fanno il ſoggetto, ſopra le quali ſi paſſaggia, non è altro che vna ſemibreue, queſta può anco ſeruire per breue, minima, & ſemiminima.

Et volendo paſſaggiare la breue, vi ne ſono notati alcuni: ma volendoſene ſeruire per ogni ſoggetto,ſi piglieranno le ſedici ſemicrome fatte per la ſemibreue,& ſi faranno crome: per la ſemibreue,come ſtanno, eccettuandone alcune da farſi di ſemiminime, che ſtanno nelle caſelle d'eſſe ſemiminime, le quali poi facendoli ſopra le minime,& ſemiminime,renderanno gratioſo cōcento,con non minore ſonorità delle gradate.

Et per paſſaggiare le minime,ſi piglieranno le quattro ſemiminime,& ſi faranno crome,& per ſemicrome,le otto crome delle ſemibreue,& per le ſemi minime,l'iſteſſe ſemiminime ſi faranno ſemicrome.

Et hauendo forſi alcuno difficultà,che non ſi poſſa conoſcere quali paſſaggi ſiano boni,hora per vna conſonanza,& hora per l'altra,& che per queſto ſi reſti di eſſercitarſi à cantare, ſonare, ò ſcriuere opere paſſaggiate: per leuare quelli che di queſto haueſſero alcun dubbio,ho fatte & ſegnate con vna crocetta (come ſi vede) ſol tre variationi,laſciando delle altre che ſi potrebbono ſegnare, per non generar confuſione.

La prima doue ſtanno nella caſella delle ſemiminime,la ſeconda nelle crome,& la terza nelle ſemicrome,le quali douunque ſi ſcriueranno,ò ſi faranno con la voce, conſoneranno con la ſpecie della ottaua,decima,& duodecima, & poſsonſi fare ſopra la breue,ſemibreue,minima, & ſemiminima con la maniera già detta, pigliandoſi quella di ſotto, di ſopra, ò nel mezo, doue dimoſtrerà la crocetta.

E contentandoſi per vn principio paſsaggiare ſolo di crome, dico che li mouimenti principali,& ordinarij,che fanno il ſoggetto per paſſaggiare, non ſono più di noue,duoi gradati, cioè mi fa, & fà mi, duoi per terza, duoi per quarta,duoi per quinta,& vna ferma, li quali in noue giorni ſi poſsono imparare,& ténerli in memoria,& in venti ò poco più eſsercitandoli ſi poſsono fare,cantando ſicuramente in ogni libro all'improuiſo.

Et per voler paſſaggiare qual ſi voglia opera, baſterà ſolo conſiderare la qualità delle note, & il ſito atto ad eſſere paſſaggiato, & poi ſecondo il loro valore, di eſſi pigliarne copia: dicendo, che ſe la voſtra nota che volete paſſaggiare ſarà breue,ſemibreue,minima, ò ſemiminima, & che dica mi fa, o altre,andate alle ſimili del libretto,& di eſſe recauatane li paſſaggi ſegnati, che conſoneranno,come hò detto,ouero pigliarete dell'altri che ſaranno forſi più vaghi,eſsendo fatti per le conſonanze del loro genere:ſeruendoſi però del diletto dell'orecchie, le quali amiche del concento,ſono maeſtre à far conoſcere il bono dal falſo,& variare, accreſcere, e ſminuire il paſſaggio, ſecondo la facilità della diſpoſitione.

Et ſe quelli ch'inſegnano, eſſercitaranno i loro ſcolari à far cantar ſeco li primi ſoggetti à battuta,oueramente dargliene cantando vna per volta alla mente di quelli ſegnati che ſon pochi,ò delli altri,con facilità,& in poco tempo ſaranno introdotti,che intoneranno, prenderanno quelli con guſto, & à poco à poco diuenteranno familiari, agili,ſicuri,& poſſeſſori con regola di tutti li ſoggetti fatti, atti al paſſaggiare ſopra tutte le note.

Et facendosi il scolare agile di voce, potrà anco acquistare da se la gratia; & sentendo altri, sarà assai più facile ad imitare, che quello che di molti anni hà cantato sicuro, come stà nel libro.

Possono ancora quelli che si dilettano di passaggiare, pigliare quattro, ò più note alla volta, di quelle che fanno il soggetto, & ponerle l'vna appresso all'altra, & poi di esse pigliarne il passaggio di crome, semicrome, ò puntate, vnendoli; & esercitandosi cantandoli alla mente, diuenteranno con prestezza agili di dispositione.

Seruono anco per quelli che vogliono esercitarsi con la viola, ò altri strumenti da fiato, con sonarli spesso, ò scriuerli con la maniera gia detta; che vsandoli, giouerà à far la mano leggiadra, l'arcata dolce, conoscere il genere del passaggio, come si scriuono, & resterà nella memoria la diuersità di essi: & hauendo sopra ciò fatta bona prattica, si possono poi dimostrare, sonandoli in compagnia all'improuiso. Et non trouando l'vt re, re mi, fa sol, & il sol la, con gl'altri, doue vorresti, che per non far maggior volume mi son ristretto solo al mi fà, per la regola delle chiaui (come hò detto) potrà ciascuno con suo commodo scriuerseli distesi, e per quelle chiaui che desiderarà.

OTHER MUSIC TITLES AVAILABLE FROM
Pro/Am Music Resources, Inc.

BIOGRAPHY

ALKAN, REISSUE *by Ronald Smith.* Vol. 1: The Enigma. Vol. 2: The Music.
BÉLA BARTÓK: His Life in Pictures and Documents *ed. by Ferenc Bónis.*
JOHN FOULDS AND HIS MUSIC: An Introduction *by Malcolm MacDonald.*
LIPATTI *by Dragos Tanasescu & Grigore Bargauanu.*
MASCAGNI: An Autobiography Compiled, Edited and Translated from Original Sources *by David Stivender.*
MAX REGER *by Gerhard Wuensch.*
MICHAEL TIPPETT, O.M.: A Celebration *edited by Geraint Lewis. Fwd. by Peter Maxwell Davies.*
MY LIFE WITH BOHUSLAV MARTINU *by Charlotte Martinu.*
PERCY GRAINGER: The Man Behind the Music *by Eileen Dorum.*
PERCY GRAINGER: The Pictorial Biography *by Robert Simon. Fwd. by Frederick Fennell.*
SORABJI: A Critical Celebration *edited by Paul Rapoport.*
VERDI AND WAGNER *by Ernö Lendvai.*
ZOLTAN KODALY: His Life in Pictures and Documents *by László Eosze.*

GENERAL SUBJECTS

AMERICAN MINIMAL MUSIC, REISSUE *by Wim Mertens. Transl. by J. Hautekiet.*
THE ANATOMY OF A NEW YORK DEBUT RECITAL *by Carol Montparker.*
THE FOLK MUSIC REVIVAL IN SCOTLAND, REISSUE *by Ailie Munro.*
KENTNER: A Symposium *edited by Harold Taylor. Fwd. by Yehudi Menuhin.*
THE MUSICAL INSTRUMENT COLLECTOR, REVISED EDITION *by J. Robert Willcutt & Kenneth R. Ball.*
MUSICOLOGY IN PRACTICE: Collected Essays by Denis Stevens *edited by Thomas P. Lewis.* Vol. 1: 1948-1970. Vol. 2: 1971-1988.
THE PIANIST'S TALENT *by Harold Taylor. Fwd. by John Ogdon.*
THE PRO/AM BOOK OF MUSIC AND MYTHOLOGY *compiled, edited & with commentaries by Thomas P. Lewis.*